SPOOKY VIBES

40 coloring pages featuring

CUTE AND COMFY COLORING BOOK FOR ADULTS, TEENS AND KIDS.

PUBLISHED IN 2024 BY ARTY AMMIE

Copyright © 2024 by Arty Ammie

50+ FREE DIGITAL COLORING PAGES!

Share your fabulous finished artwork with us!
Join our Facebook group to let your creativity shine.
Scan the QR code to join the group:

LEARN HOW TO COLOR!

Visit our social media and get inspired!

@arty.ammie

COLOR YOUR WAY TO HAPPY!

Life can get busy, and sometimes we all need a little pick-me-up! Art is a fun and creative way to relax, express ourselves, and find some inner peace.

PAPER CHOICE

To keep our coloring book affordable with the paper options available on Amazon, we've opted for standard-quality paper. While this paper might experience some bleeding with certain pens or markers, you can easily prevent this! Simply place a blank sheet of thicker paper behind the page you're coloring. We appreciate your understanding and hope you have a blast coloring yourself happy!

SHARE YOUR ARTWORKS

We've been thrilled to see countless pages come alive with color by creative artists like you since launching our Coloring Books on Amazon. When you leave feedback on Amazon, feel free to share pictures and celebrate your unique creations! We can't wait to see your masterpieces on social media, too.

CONNECT WITH US!

For any concerns, please feel free to contact us at: artyammie18@gmail.com

This Book belongs to:

Color test page

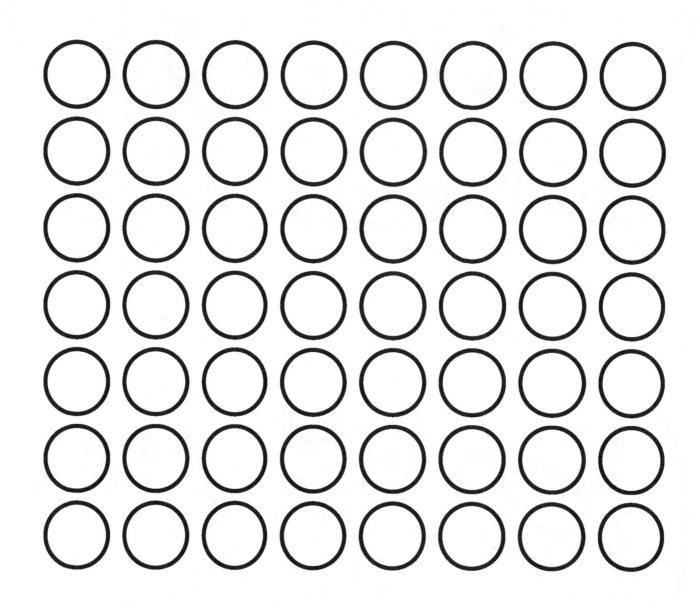

TO OUR VALUED READER,

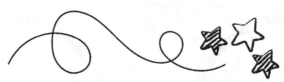

Thank you for choosing and investing in this book. Your support means the world to us, and it is your encouragement that allows us to continue creating and sharing our passion for meaningful and inspiring content. This book is a culmination of countless hours of dedication, creativity, and hard work, and we hope it brings as much joy and fulfillment to you as it did to us in its creation.

WE WOULD LOVE TO HEAR FROM YOU!

Your thoughts and experiences are incredibly important to us. We invite you to share your journey with us and become a part of our growing community. Connect with us on social media and leave a review on Amazon page. Your insights help us to improve and continue providing you with the best possible products.

CONNECT WITH US!

For any concerns, please feel free to contact us at:

artyammie18@gmail.com

FOR MORE BOOKS,
SCAN QR CODE AND
FOLLOW US ON
AMAZON!

Made in the USA
Las Vegas, NV
08 October 2024

96532963R00050